TELESCOPE HUNTERS!
WHAT TO LOOK FOR IN YOUR TELESCOPE FOR KIDS

CHILDREN'S ASTROPHYSICS & SPACE SCIENCE BOOKS

PROFESSOR GUSTO
EDUCATIONAL & INFORMATIVE BOOKS FOR CHILDREN
(PRE-K / K-12)

Seeing through a telescope could be an enjoyable activity. You can see far things up close.

Depending on the telescope that you use, you can even see the stars, the moon and the planets, too!

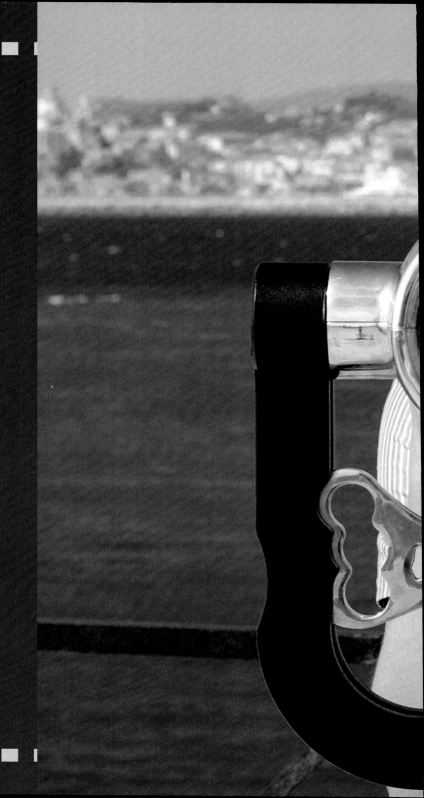

What are
the things to
consider in
choosing a
telescope?

First, look at the aperture size. The aperture is the most important feature of a telescope.

The larger the aperture the brighter and clearer the images get. However, a big aperture also means a large telescope.

Second, determine the magnification through the telescope's eyepiece.

Magnification is still dependent on aperture. High magnification is considered important, but we have to consider the aperture.

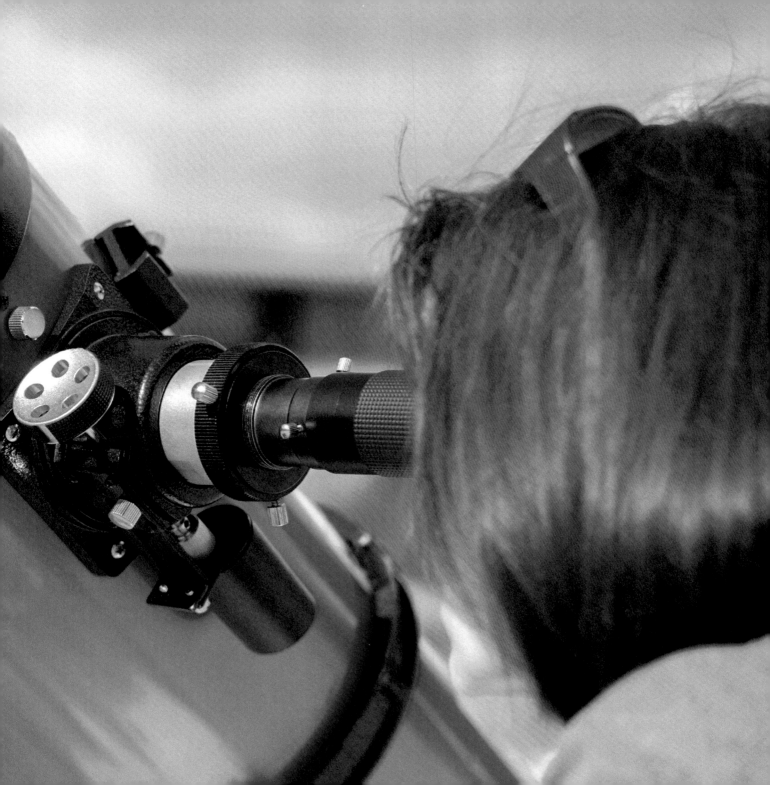

A high magnification eyepiece does not blend well with a low aperture telescope. That is why some telescopes have more than one eyepiece.

Durability has to be considered, too. Many telescopes are readily available for future astronomers and for future telescope hunters.

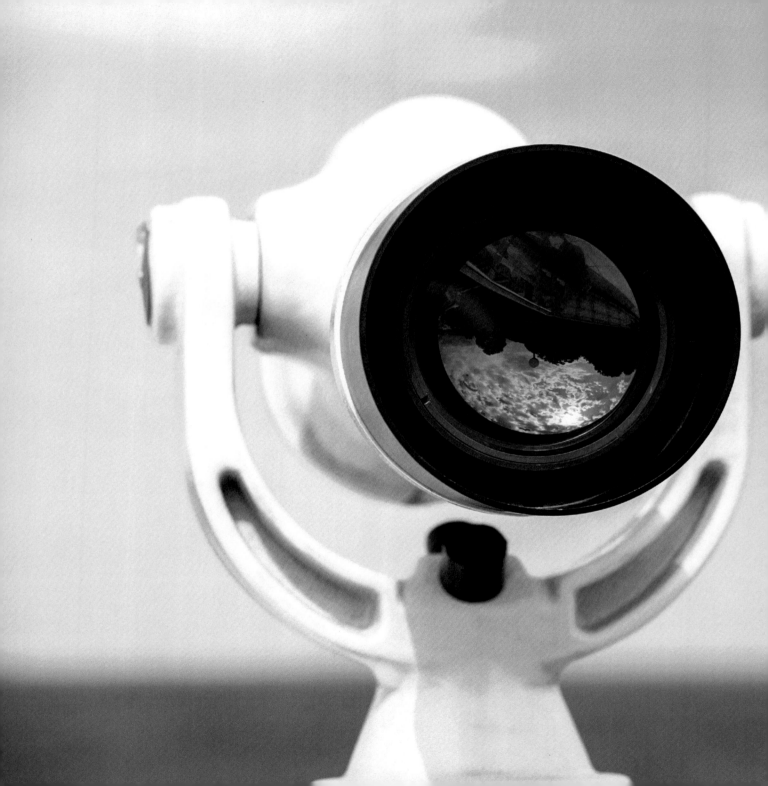

It is noted that telescopes come in different sizes, prices and shapes.

Whatever you choose, one thing is for sure - you can see many amazing things through a telescope!

What's the
difference
between a
reflector and
a refractor?

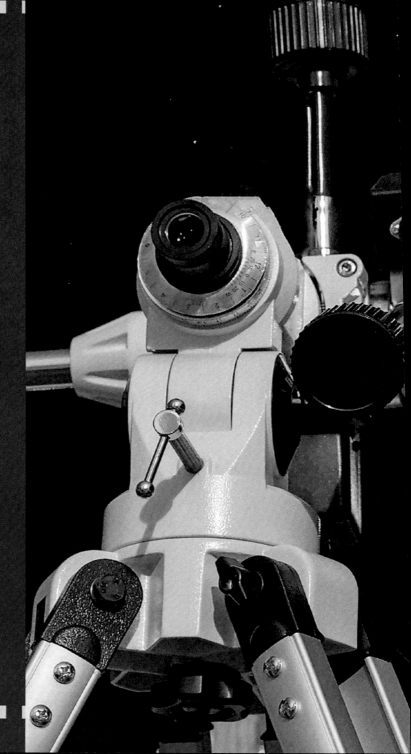

For celestial viewing, a reflector telescope is used.

Kids usually prefer to have a refractor telescope because it allows them to view the stars and the moon better. It gives them the opportunity to view land space.

Do you want to see Jupiter?

Jupiter outshines every star because it is considered as the King of the Planets.

If you see it in your telescope, you will also witness its many moons. This is possible with larger telescopes or those with 6-inch mirrors or lens.

To achieve maximum fun and enjoyment, be sure that you set up your telescope outdoors. Be patient. Most astronomical objects may be dim at first, but with the right adjustments, you should be able to see them just fine.

Should you be asking mommy for a telescope? Maybe you should!

Made in the USA
Middletown, DE
05 December 2016